Hopscotch Love

A Family Treasury of Love Poems

BY Nikki Grimes

ILLUSTRATED BY

Melodye Benson Rosales

Lothrop, Lee & Shepard Books ♥ *Morrow*

NEW YORK

Contents

Hopscotch Love 4

Sweet Tooth 6

Words 7

Why I Hate Jamel 8

Eye-Luv-U 10

Miss Lee 11

Marcus Toussaint 12

Sister Love 13

Christmas Valentine 14

Uncle Willis 16

Pineapple Surprise 18

Do Like Malcolm 20

Medgar & Myrlie 22

Juicy-Fruit Love 24

Mr. Lester 26

True Love Blues 28

Secret Love 29

The Gift 30

No Excuses 32

A Little Understanding 34

Mother Love 36

Sweethearts Dance 38

Hopscotch Love

Jerome
is gone and still my feet
carry me
to his used-to-be street.
And there
I sketch a hopscotch board
with chalk
as broken as my heart.
And in
the squares where numbers go
I scrawl
his name in curlicues,
then play
hopscotch, but not alone—
I share
each square with my Jerome.

Sweet Tooth

HI, KISHA

If you're reading this
then you musta found it
in your backpack
where I stuck it.
Don't worry—
I didn't take anything.

LISTEN:

my mom said
girls like chocolate
and I figured
she should know.
S-o-o-o-o-o
HERE'S A HERSHEY BAR
WITH NUTS
WHICH IS WHAT I AM
ABOUT YOU.

p.s.
Imade thiscard myself
doyou likeit?

Tyrell

Words

Sugar
Honey
Sweetie Pie
Shortcake
Cupcake
Sweet Dumplin'
Chocolate Drop—
Seems to me
That love
Might lead
To cavities.

Why I Hate Jamel

Firstly,
he steals the beads
from my braids
and slips them
in his pockets
like it's some joke
that only he
finds funny.

Secondly,
he snakes his tongue
out at me
whenever his
childish friends
catch him grinning
in my direction.

Thirdly,
he crashes into me
on the stairway
ten times a day
instead of saying hello
as if he doesn't know
how mad this makes me.

But today,
he asked me to be
his valentine
and said I have
outrageously pretty eyes.
So even though
I mostly hate Jamel,
I love him otherwise.

Eye-Luv-U

I was sittin' in class
when Dante come passin' by,
peekin' in my notebook
all squinty-eyed.
I shut that book so fast
I thought his head would spin.
But he's been grinnin' ever since, so
I guess I didn't close it fast enough.
He musta seen that stuff I wrote
about "Dante + me, 4-ever."

Miss Lee

Miss Lee appeared
Just as I took my seat.

She saw my lacy
Valentine in chalk.

She reached for her
Eraser instantly.

I held my breath
Convinced my heart would stop.

But then she turned
To face the class and smiled—

And left my blackboard
Valentine untouched.

Marcus Toussaint

Marcus is conspicuous
>   most everywhere we go.
Yet he's not keen on being tall.
>   I'm his best friend. I know.
His height sure comes in handy, though,
>   when tough kids bother me.
Marcus shows up, and they run off.
>   I'm just glad they can't see
How scared Marcus Toussaint is—
>   he's only brave outside.
But I can always count on him
>   to help protect my hide.

Sister Love

My sister and I dream of adoption—someday.
In the dream, we're never apart.
Then this nice lady comes to the group home
With a girl-shaped hole in her heart.

The nice lady seemed to like Kari and me
But she only had spare room for one.
Her home was fairly small, she said,
And she already had a son.

My age was closest to her boy's
So she asked if I wanted to go.
I squeezed my sister's trembling hand
And whispered, "Thanks, but no."

Christmas Valentine

I asked Mama
What she wanted
For Christmas.
"Honey," she said,
"All I want is you."
But I'm way too big
To fit under the tree.
So, when she
Wasn't looking
I snuck into
Her sewing room
For scraps of velvet,
Gold ribbon, and lace
And got tracing paper
From out of my desk
And grabbed the glue.
Then two days later
I gave Mama
Her very first
Christmas valentine.
I'd pasted my picture
Smack in the middle.
And I could swear a little tear
Ran down her cheek
When I said,
"Merry Christmas, Mama."

Uncle Willis

Aunt Anna calls herself
An old biddy.
Says even her memories
Have gray hair. All I know
Is that her shuffle
Is slow and wobbly
And her smooth brow
Is the only part of her
That doesn't ache these days.
Her bones beg her
To stay in bed till noon.
But she never misses lunch
'Cause Uncle Willis
Knows a thing or two
About cooking.
He bangs around
What used to be
Aunt Anna's kitchen,
Heats her up
A can of soup
And stirs it with a spoon
They bought together.

He carries the food to her
On a tray
And sometimes
Has to feed her
The way
My mom
Used to feed me.
Ever since Aunt Anna
Took sick last year
I been hearing people
Tell Uncle Willis
He should up and go
Find him somebody
Who doesn't need
Such special care,
Somebody who is
Easier to love.
But Uncle says
Easy love
Is not the only kind
Or maybe even the best.
And either way
Aunt Anna is his life
And his love for her
Is not a habit
He plans on breaking.

Pineapple Surprise

Grandma wasn't much for hugging.
She was entirely too frail
to give me piggyback rides
and moved too slow
for hide-and-seek.
But sometimes,
while I played alone,
she would magically appear
with pineapple upside-down cake,
which took considerable trouble to make:

Honey-glazed pineapple rings
clinging to the bottom—
or was it the top?
Maraschino cherries pop-
ping with tooth tingling
tangy sweetness,
two thick layers of buttery,
gooey, scrumptiously chewy,
pineapple-licious yellow cake
baked for nobody else but me.

Do Like Malcolm

Daddy loves
To quote Malcolm.
Speechifyin'
Mama calls it.
Today at breakfast
He gave a lecture
On L-O-V-E
And pointed out
How Malcolm said
Real love was
For every day
And not just
The special one
Marked on
The calendar
In February.
Then Daddy said
"Who needs roses
And love notes

Anyway?"
Mama was quiet
But I never am
So I said "Daddy
I read this book
In school
On Malcolm X
And I think
You should do
Like Malcolm did
For Mrs. Malcolm.
Write Mama some
Mushy love poems
And hide them
In a dresser drawer.
But make sure
She can find them."
And Mama looked up
From her coffee cup
And gave Daddy
The biggest smile
Which told me
Them poems must be
A pretty good idea.

Medgar & Myrlie

Medgar rarely
spoke his feelings
though his Myrlie
owned his heart.

So he brought her
bare-root roses
that she planted
like their love.

Medgar's soul now
rests assured that
death cannot up-
root love's seed.

As in life, their
love still blossoms
watered by her
tears, his blood.

Civil-rights leader Medgar Evers was slain in 1963. Since his
death, Myrlie Evers, his widow, has continued the fight for
equality and has remained devoted to the memory of his life
and their love.

Juicy-Fruit Love

My mouth was
Dry as dust
So I searched
My jeans pocket
For something good
To chew.
But first
My fingers had to
Wade through
Jujubes
Balls of lint
A handful
Of red-hots
One dirt-encrusted
Gummi Bear
And the rubber spider
That sent my sister
Screaming from
My room one night.

Then—yes!
I found it:
One last stick
Of Juicy Fruit.
I licked my lips
Started removing
The silver wrapper
And then
SHE showed up
Smiling that smile.
Brown eyes locked on
My sugary treasure
And before
My brain knew
What my heart
Was up to
I'd reached out
Handed her
My last stick of gum
And *thanked* her
For accepting it.
So I suppose
There's really
No hope for me now.

Mr. Lester

I used to feel ugly
Till Sis started sending me
To Lester's Bar-B-Q Pit
For hot ribs and greens.
Now, soon as I burst
Through that
Restaurant door
Hungry for flattery
Mr. Lester starts.
"Hey, Good-Lookin'.
How's my girl today?
You're gettin' to be
Mighty pretty," he'll say.
I giggle every time.
"Now you go easy
On them boys, you hear?"
Go easy how? I ask.
"Don't you go breakin'
All they hearts."
Oh, Mr. Lester
Stop! I say,
That ugly feeling
Long-gone away.
But he goes right on
Teasing me.
And I go right on
Loving it.

True Love Blues

Love means putting others first—
That's what love's about.
Lord says you gotta put me first
'Cause that's what love's about.
But the way you hog that apple pie
Proves you still ain't figured that out.

Secret Love

Dear Diary,
You're still at home, so I'm
writing in my loose-leaf book
if that's okay. The thing is this:
You'd think with all the guys
we have in school, a few
would slip me heart-shaped mints,
a lollipop or two. A postcard
would be nice—I think I'm due.
In fact, I rate at least one
imitation velvet valentine.
But wait! What's this . . .

(Dear Diary,
Never mind.)

The Gift

Outside a flower shop, Jewel waits.
Her school bus will soon come.
John Paul, the cute boy next to her,
Nervously starts to hum.

He holds a rosebud in his hand.
He twirls the stem and breaks it,
But still, he offers it to Jewel,
Who giggles first, then takes it.

She gently lays the store-bought rose
Inside her English book.
Ten times that day she eyes her gift,
And sighs with each long look.

No Excuses

My last report card
Was smudged with
Nervous sweat
& red ink
Which practically
Screamed failure.
Daddy sighed
At the C–
Groaned at the D
& burned his
Disappointment
Into me with
One long look.
"Son," he said,
"We both know

You can do better."
Which is true.
So I studied
My sneakers
& mumbled,
"Sorry, Dad."
"Next term
Try harder,"
He said.
"Meantime quit
Looking like
You just lost
Your best friend.
Now, I'm not wild
About your grades,
But I don't need
A good excuse
To love you."

A Little Understanding

. . . And God bless Aunt Edna
for inviting me to rummage through
her dresser drawer of memories:

    A ring of tarnished keys
    to nowhere I could find;

    A faded fan from My Redeemer
    urging the recently bereaved
    to consider Miller's Funeral Home
    for their loved one's final farewell;

    A linen handkerchief
    still boasting
    Uncle Abe's initials;

    And a photograph
    yellow with years—
    A portrait of two
    sepia-toned Kewpie dolls.

The girl-bride wore
her dark caramel beauty
cinched in folds
of white satin and lace.

    The promise of Forever
    beaming from familiar
    dream-glazed eyes and face—

No wonder
Daddy loved her.

Mother Love

Mom says
She remembers
The night
I came running
Into her room
In bare feet
Wearing faded
Superman pajamas
Tears chasing
Each other
Down my cheeks
Because I'd had
A scary dream
About drowning.
She remembers

How I dove under
The quilt & curled
Into the curve
Of her back
Where I slept
Like a baby
& how I
Tickled her awake
The next day
& sprayed her
With laughter.
I don't understand
How she could cram
So many details
Into this memory
When all I know
Is that one night
I cried & she
Was there.

Sweethearts Dance

He pulls her close
She strokes his face
Their thoughts fly to
Their starting place

The Sweethearts Dance
The day they met
He still remembers
She can't forget

The music plays
Just like before
The graying sweethearts
Young once more
Whirl and dance
Across the floor

For my father, James Grimes,
the first man to steal my heart.
—*N.G.*

♥

For all my loved ones,
thank you for being there.
—*M.B.R.*

"Christmas Valentine" first appeared in the anthology *Hold Christmas in Your Heart: African-American Songs, Poems, and Stories for the Holidays,* compiled by Cheryl Hudson, published by Cartwheel Books, Scholastic, Inc., 1995. "Pineapple Surprise" first appeared in the anthology *Food Fight,* compiled by Michael Rosen, published by Harcourt Brace & Co., Inc., 1996.

Pastel and Prismacolor pencils on acrylic and oil paints
were used for the full-color illustrations.
The text type is 13-point Berkeley Oldstyle Medium.

Text copyright © 1999 by Nikki Grimes
Illustrations copyright © 1999 by Melodye Benson Rosales

Published by Lothrop, Lee & Shepard Books
an imprint of Morrow Junior Books
a division of William Morrow and Company, Inc.
1350 Avenue of the Americas, New York, NY 10019
www.williammorrow.com

Printed in the United States of America.

10 9 8 7 6 5 4 3 2 1

Library of Congress Cataloging-in-Publication Data
Grimes, Nikki.
Hopscotch love: a family treasury of love poems / by Nikki Grimes;
illustrated by Melodye Benson Rosales.
p. cm.
Summary: A collection of more than twenty poems speaking
of different kinds of love.
ISBN 0-688-15667-3
1. Children's poetry, American.   2. Afro-Americans—Juvenile poetry.
3. Love—Juvenile poetry.   [1. Love—Poetry.   2. Afro-Americans—Poetry.
3. American poetry.]   I. Rosales, Melodye Benson, ill.   II. Title.
PS3557.R489982H67 1999   811'.54—DC21   98-21310   CIP AC